# Stunt Jets

Written by Catherine Veitch
Photographed by Will Amlot

## Contents

**Collins**

Look at the stunt jets. Get set for lift off!

# You will need:

sheets

# A swift jet

Bend the sheet like this.

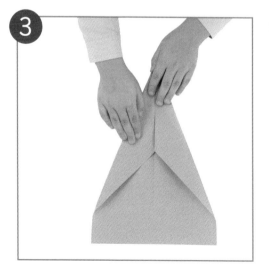

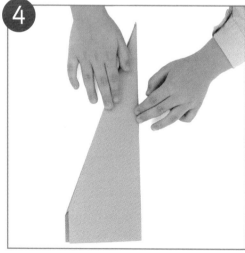

# Press down the wings.

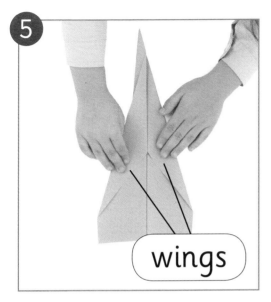

wings

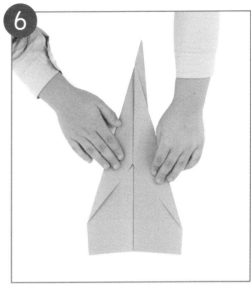

7 Can you zoom
and spin?

# A stunt jet

Flatten the sheet like this.

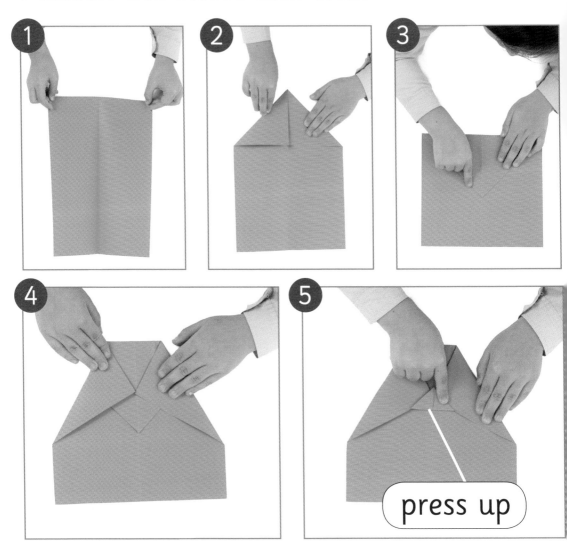

press up

# Then bend out the wings.

**8** See it twist and flip.

# A moth jet

Press out the sheet like this.

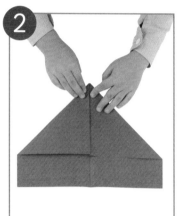

# To finish, tuck out the wings.

**6**

**7**

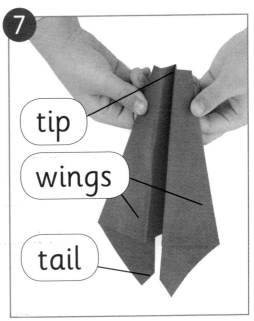

tip

wings

tail

**8** Buzz off ...

# A griffin jet

Bend the sheet like this.

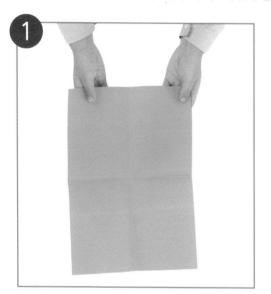

# Turn the top of the sheet.

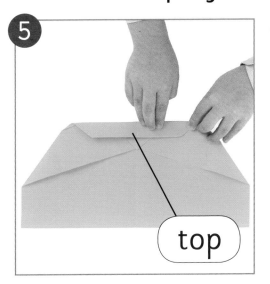

**5**

top

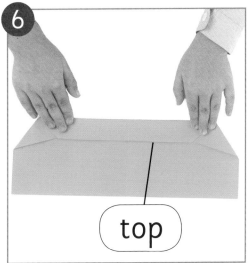

**6**

top

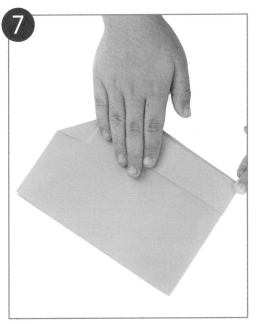

**7**

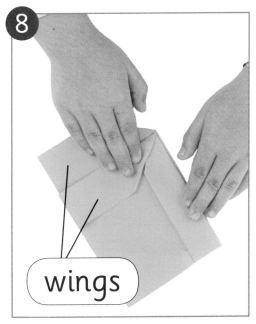

**8**

wings

# Next, bend the bottom.

9

bend

10 Can it dart and drift?

# Jet target

Cut targets in a big sheet of card.
Can you get the jets in?

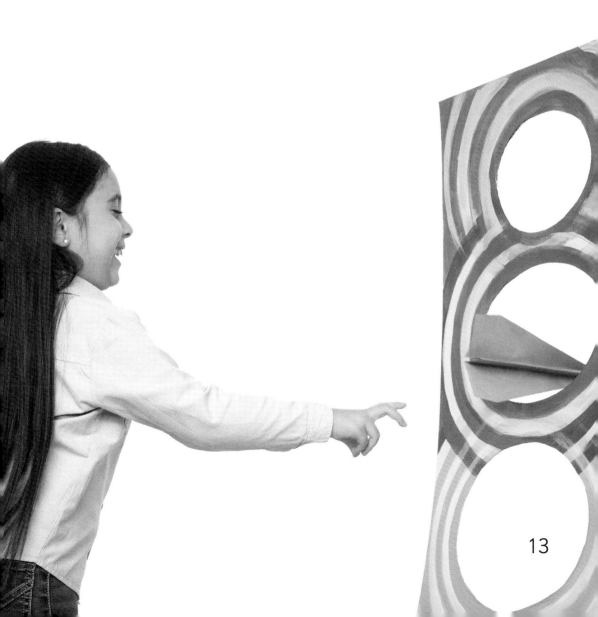

# The jets

## Swift jet

## Stunt jet

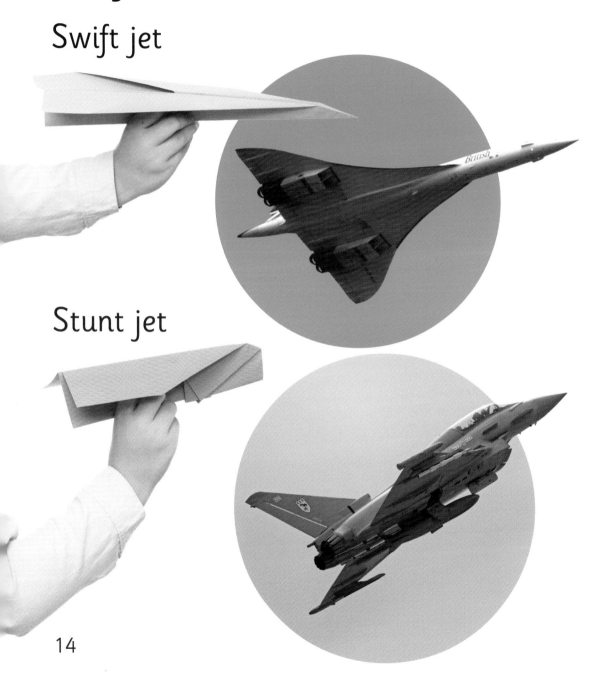

# Moth jet

# Griffin jet

# After reading

**Letters and Sounds:** Phase 4

**Word count:** 114

Focus on adjacent consonants with short vowel phonemes, e.g. /s/ /t/ /u/ /n/ /t/

**Common exception words:** to, the, you

**Curriculum links (EYFS):** Expressive arts and design: Exploring and using media and materials

**Curriculum links (National Curriculum, Year 1):** Design and technology: make, technical knowledge

**Early learning goals:** Listening and attention: children listen attentively in a range of situations; Understanding: answer 'how' and 'why' questions about their experiences and in response to stories or events; Reading: read and understand simple sentences, use phonic knowledge to decode regular words and read them aloud accurately, read some common irregular words, demonstrate understanding when talking with others about what they have read.

**National Curriculum learning objectives:** Spoken language: listen and respond appropriately to adults and their peers; Reading/word reading: apply phonic knowledge and skills as the route to decode words, read aloud accurately books that are consistent with their developing phonic knowledge and that do not require them to use other strategies to work out words, read accurately by blending sounds in unfamiliar words containing GPCs that have been taught; Reading/comprehension: understand ... books they can already read accurately and fluently ... by: checking that the text makes sense to them as they read and correcting inaccurate reading

## Developing fluency

- Your child may enjoy hearing you read the book. Model reading the instructions, following the steps clearly.
- You may wish to read alternate instructions, encouraging your child to read with expression.

## Phonic practice

- Practise reading adjacent consonants. Model sounding out the following word, saying each of the sounds quickly and clearly. Then blend the sounds together. s/t/u/n/t
- Ask your child to say each of the sounds in the following words, pointing to the letter as they make the sound.

  bend                  flip                  drift                  twist

- Now ask your child if they can read each of the words without sounding them out.